IMAGES OF
EXETER

Express & Echo

IMAGES OF
EXETER

The
Breedon Books
Publishing Company
Derby

Published in Great Britain by
The Breedon Books Publishing Company Limited
Breedon House, 44 Friar Gate, Derby, DE1 1DA
1994

ISBN 1 873626 71 1

Printed and bound by Butler and Tanner Limited, Frome and London.
Jackets printed by BDC Printing Services Limited of Derby

Contents

Introduction

No better symbol of Exeter's 2,000 years of history could be found than the discovery some years ago of the highly impressive remains of a Roman legionary bath house and basilica.

These were unearthed directly in front of the city's 1,100-year-old Cathedral after the nearby church of St Mary Major had been demolished. While debate continues about whether or not to make the Roman bath house into a tourist attraction, it is estimated that as much as 20 per cent of the original Roman town lies beneath the Cathedral, the Bishop's Palace, the Palace Gate Convent and other properties near the Cathedral.

Exeter, standing in a commanding position above the river Exe, is the Devon capital: many consider it also to be the provincial capital of the south-western peninsula of England. it has a wealth of historical records. The city was named by Ptolemy as Isca Dumnoniorum after the name of the British tribes that inhabited the region.

The Danes captured Exeter in 876 and spent the winter there. In 1001 the Danes were back again and being unable to take Exeter burned the nearby villages of Pinhoe and Broadclyst. Since 1050 Exeter has been the seat of a bishopric; there has been a castle (Rougemont) there since 1086 and a Guildhall in the High Street since at least the twelfth century. The history of its mayors begins very shortly after those of London. Moreover from the tenth to the eighteenth century it was an important port – at one time the third or fourth most significant in the country. Its quayside area made an ideal location for scenes in the *Onedin Line* TV serial and in the same area there is an impressive maritime museum.

In 1086 Exeter was besieged and taken by William the Conqueror who built a castle there. It was again besieged in 1137 by King Stephen for three months. In 1469 it again held out successfully for 12 days against another siege by the Yorkists; and was once more besieged by Perkin Warbeck in 1497. A more important siege occurred in 1549 at the time of the Prayer Book Rebellion. And in the Civil War Exeter was twice besieged but no major battles took place there.

Exeter was one of several Devon centres which prospered in

A view of the St Leonard's area of Exeter from above the city Basin in 1900.

6

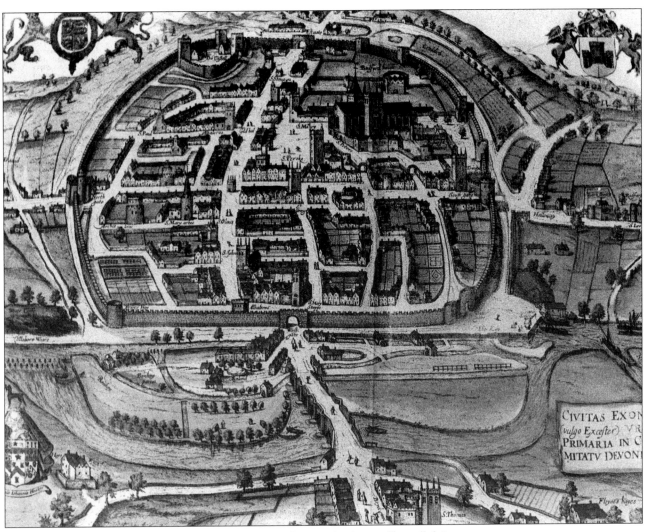

A classic impression of Exeter when it was still a walled city.

the heyday of the wool trade in the late seventeenth and early eighteenth century and Topsham, an ancient port incorporated into Exeter several years ago, still has the nostalgic atmosphere of a once flourishing maritime town. Exeter still has many old buildings of interest to visitors and residents – including the Cathedral, the Guildhall, St Nicholas Priory and Tuckers' Hall. Its famous 'house that moved', the remains of an old Exe bridge, the area around St Mary Arches and the well-preserved Quay area give more than a hint of how the old city once looked.

One of the more unusual features to attract visitors to Exeter is its underground passages – part of a surviving medieval system to bring water in from outside the city walls.

It has for centuries, because of its geographical location, been a secular, religious and cultural centre. Routes from all over the vast county of Devon converge on it – a fact which in the 1960s led to enormous traffic jams that regularly made national headlines. The building of the M5 motorway and the major road improvements have greatly eased the problem.

Exeter suffered severely at the hands of Hitler's bombers and large areas of the medieval city were destroyed. All of its picturesque old gateways have gone and extensive rebuilding, not always to the best of designs, has taken place. But many gracious older areas remain; and there is now an interesting blend of old and new city centre buildings as well as two

bridges instead of one over the river Exe. The bridges were constructed as part of a massive flood alleviation scheme following disastrous floods in 1960.

The city has two major industrial estates and currently there is considerable expansion of the city on its eastern fringe with large superstores and offices being built. Yet miraculously Exeter still retains much of its appeal as a city in a county setting. And from many places in it there are glimpses of the lush Devon countryside – a fact which underlines its historic importance as a focal point for a huge agricultural hinterland.

The city is a major legal and administrative centre with both Devon County Council and Exeter City Council offices within its boundaries.

Not everybody in Exeter welcomes all the changes. There are regrets that the Theatre Royal, where Henry Irving (and Tony Hancock) once played, is no more. Others think that the Guildhall centre, built after years of interminable haggling over how the area should be developed, is a brash modern intrusion.

The city has a University on a magnificent campus and many modern shops, buskers and market traders, and for contrast there is still the charm of Rougemont Gardens, the quaintness of Gandy Street, the elegance of Southernhay and the architectural appeal of Cathedral Close.

In such places a sense of the past mingles dynamically with

the present. It is one of Exeter's many qualities that recently gained it an accolade as a city with a high quality of life.

The old and delightfully scenic Exeter canal is now used only by pleasure craft though it once carried commercial shipping. On either side of the Exe estuary are seaside towns that are favourites with both residents and visitors while there are eight million visits made to the Dartmoor National Park every year – quite a large proportion of them by local people.

Appropriately from the point of this book one of the first photographers in England – Richard Beard – set up business in the city in 1841 and since then there have been many thousands of pictures taken of Exeter's buildings, people and events and of the Devon towns and resorts whose history is linked with the city.

From the files of Exeter's evening newspaper the *Express and Echo* and from many readers who have sent the newspaper interesting old pictures and from a number of my own photographs this book has been compiled.

Tim Williams

Exeter Buildings

The old Exeter market in 1923.

The window tax probably accounted for this bleak view in old Bartholomew Street, Exeter.

9

This old bank on the corner of Exeter High Street and Bedford Street was replaced after the blitz.

A rare picture of Coombe Street taken from Quay Hill in 1930.

A wintry scene in Rosebarn Lane, Exeter in 1964 before large scale housing development in the area had taken place.

THE EXETER HOTEL WITH A HISTORY

(PROPRIETOR: L. J. Searle)

" The Turk's Head " Hotel, next to the Guildhall, has been open for 650 years.

"THE TURK'S HEAD."

In the year 1289 the City Authorities granted the right to the then owners to lean a beam against the wall of the Guildhall for the payment of one penny per year (document still preserved in the Guildhall).

In the reign of Charles II., one penny was considered insufficient and consequently increased to twopence and is payable to-day. In 1569 " The Turk's Head " Hotel was sold for four score pounds, yearly rental value declared at four pounds ten shillings and ten shillings per year was payable to Her Sovereign Lady Queen Elizabeth.

Original document in the Museum, copy in the " Turk's Head " Hotel.

Experts have discovered that two of the walls in the cellar date back to 1310 and 1330 respectively.

Dickens, the great English Author, found the original of his " Fat Boy " in Pickwick Papers as " Boots " at " The Turk's Head " Hotel.

As a House of Refreshment, " The Turk's Head " still carries out ancient traditions in catering for " Snacks " and " Grills " to suit everyone's palate.

The Proprietor welcomes Visitors from all parts of the World.

This card seems to date from 1939. The text says that "The Turk's Head" next to Exeter Guildhall had been open for 650 years. It recalls that in 1289 the city authorities granted the right to then owners of the pub (which still has the same name today) to lean a beam against the wall of the Guildhall for the payment for one penny a year. This was increased to two pence in the reign of Charles II. Charles Dickens found the original of his 'Fat Boy' in Pickwick Papers at the pub.

Whipton, now a busy Exeter suburb, in quieter days.

Pinafore dresses and knickerbockers were the order of the day in this old picture of the main road through Pinhoe in the days of horse transport.

Exeter youngsters play peek-a-boo round a statue of Richard Hooker back in 1960.

The Acland Hotel, Exeter, in the 1930s.

*A leaning tree in the heart of
Exeter in 1960.*

A students Rag Day parade in Exeter in the early sixties.

Powderham Park in the nineteenth century with a view of Exmouth across the Exe estuary.

The old railway bridge at Tiverton to the south of the town. A massive new relief road is being built in the area.

This 1951 picture gives some idea of the amount of reconstruction that had to be done in Exeter after the blitz. In those days cars could be parked anywhere with no charge.

Small shops in Goldsmith Street, Exeter, in 1963. They have since been replaced by a modern shopping precinct.

Whipton residents pose for the cameraman with no fear of being knocked over by traffic.

No fear of traffic at Cullompton in days gone by.

The Admiral Vernon pub at Alphington in the days of horse transport.

Old fishermen's cottages at Monmouth Hill in Topsham in 1961.

Nadderwater near Exeter many years ago.

Rosebarn Lane, less than a mile from the centre of Exeter, in the 1930s.

Longbrook Street, Exeter in the days before cars dominated the scene.

Southernhay, Exeter in 1962.

One of Exeter's treasured old street gas lamps at North Street, Heavitree in 1957.

The old Royal Devon and Exeter hospital around 1910.

A grandiose entrance to the old baths that used to be in Exeter's Southernhay.

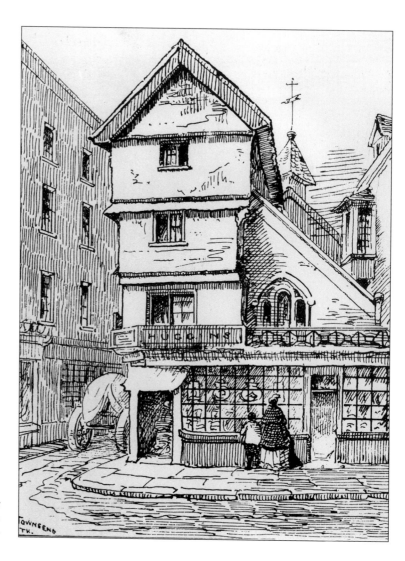

*A long since vanished scene
near Allhallows Church,
Exeter.*

*St Sidwell's Church, Exeter,
in the days before the blitz.*

*1906 in the Strand at
Topsham.*

Near the old Lime Kilns at Countess Wear, Exeter.

A multi-storey car park – one of several in Exeter – now occupies part of the site of these buildings pictured in 1964.

Below: A secular use for All Hallows Church in Bartholomew Street, Exeter about half a century ago.

Two Exeter buildings as seen by an artist.

A big new roundabout was made at the Fountain, Exeter, in 1963.

Lloyds Bank occupied these premises for thirty years: from 1912 to 1942 when they were burnt down.

Countess Wear bridge, Exeter as it was in the early twentieth century.

Looking distinctly seedy, this was Exeter's Paul Street many years ago.

One of Exeter's old gateways.

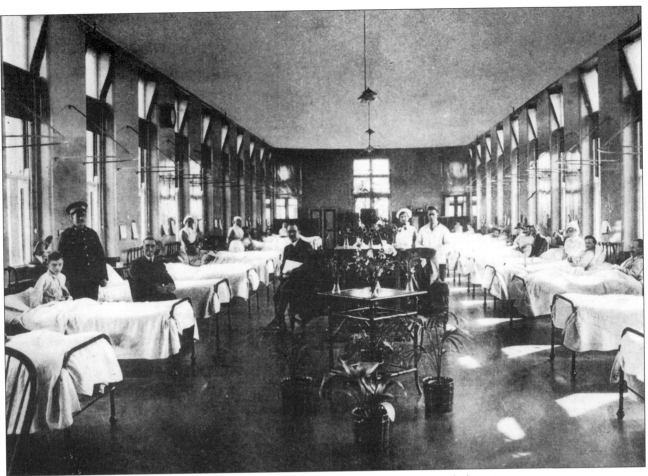

Dean Clarke ward at the Royal Devon and Exeter hospital as it was early this century.

Busy shoppers at St George's Hall market, Exeter in 1967.

Not a car in sight in this old photo of Whipton.

Eastgate made an imposing entrance to old Exeter.

An old print of Exeter's Bury Meadow and St David's Church – subsequently replaced by a new building.

Sidwell Street, Exeter about 1889.

Athelstan's Tower is a feature of Exeter's Rougemont Gardens.

Exe bridge in 1960, Cowick Street is on the right.

Church Street, Heavitree is in the foreground for this 1965 aerial view which shows the then new Royal Devon and Exeter hospital in the top left.

Bedford Street and Princesshay, Exeter in 1961.

Old Exe bridge at the bottom right in 1960. It was soon to be blamed as one of the causes of a major flood disaster.

This statue of General Sir Redvers Buller was unveiled in Exeter in 1905.

The funeral of General Sir Redvers Buller.

An auction sale notice from 1853.

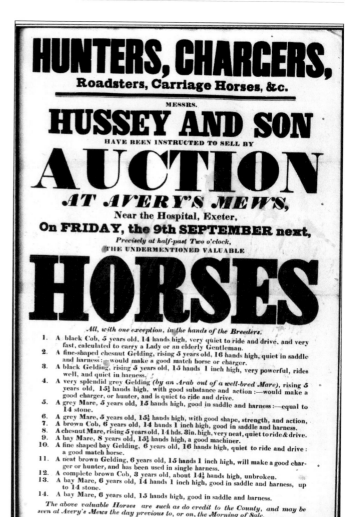

Below: One of Exeter's vanished buildings.

Environmental Health Officers were undreamt of when this picture was taken at the corner of Sidwell Street and Summerland Street, Exeter.

Below: Long horns and flat caps at Exeter Cattle Market in 1936.

*Celebrations in the main street at Topsham
on Coronation Day in 1953.*

*A graphic illustration from
the "History of Cholera" in
Exeter.*

The theme for this old Exeter pageant at Bury Meadow was a clash between the Romans and the Britons.

This was the 1910 scene at the proclamation King George V at the junction of Belmont Road and Sidwell Street.

King George VI receiving the sword of state from the Mayor of Exeter Ald. J.G.R.Orchard on the arrival of the Royal party at St David's Station.

A crowd turned out to watch a fire in Queen Street, Exeter in 1910.

Exeter University has a magnificent campus. This was taken in the spring of 1969.

Below: Exeter Technical College is on the left of this 1968 picture.

A novel means of rescue for this old Tudor House. It was put in a timber frame and moved to a new site when Exeter's inner by-pass was being made 30 odd years ago.

A 1910 picture of Cornish's butcher's shop in New Bridge Street, Exeter.

The Queen and Prince Philip on a visit to Exeter in 1958.

An archaeological dig in progress in the area of Exeter once known as the Golden Heart – now a shopping precinct.

By 1968 much of blitzed Exeter was sporting some new buildings. The tall white building on the right is now Debenhams store.

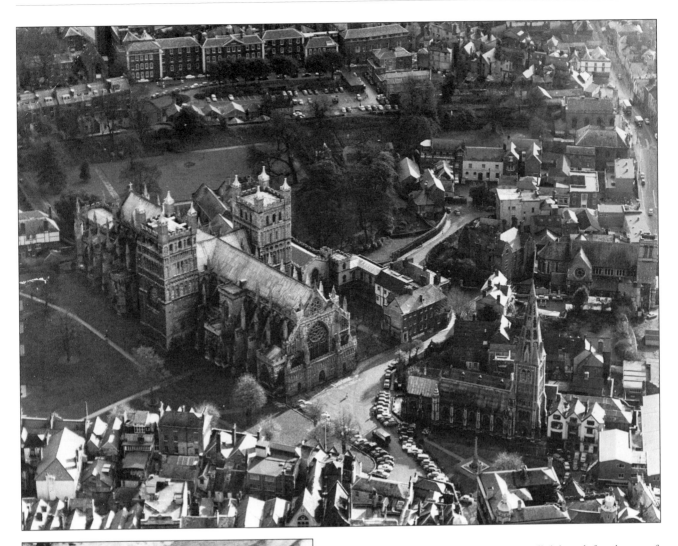

The church on the right of this picture was pulled down before the start of excavations in front of Exeter Cathedral.

Old timbers and old steps at picturesque Stepcote Hill, Exeter.

A steeplejack at work on the chimney of the Royal Devon and Exeter hospital in 1970.

An Exeter City Brewery drayhorse at the turn of the century.

A Barbara Hepworth sculpture in front of Exeter University buildings.

Early morning mist over Exeter's Duryard valley – once a Royal deer forest.

Exeter Guildhall and High Street before the days of trams or cars.

A patriotic propaganda card from 1914.

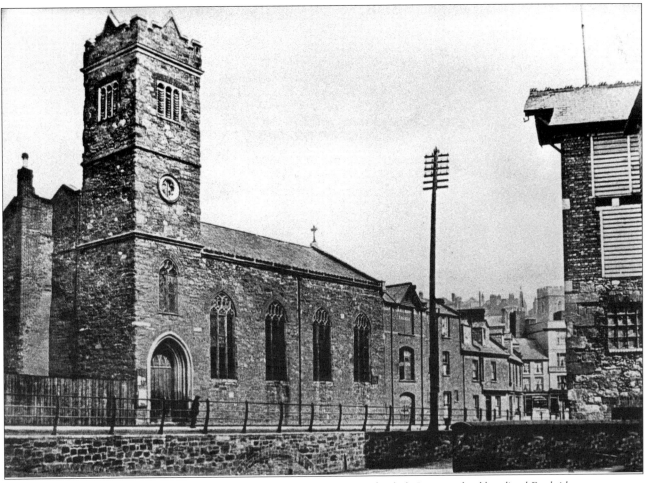

Now a picturesque ruin, this is how St Edmund's Church, Exeter, used to look. It is near the old medieval Exe bridge.

Exeter Cattle Market in 1898.

Topsham has changed little since 1960 when this picture was taken. Much of the town is a conservation area.

Once a famous coaching inn, Exeter's New London Hotel was pulled down in 1936 and replaced by a cinema which has now also gone.

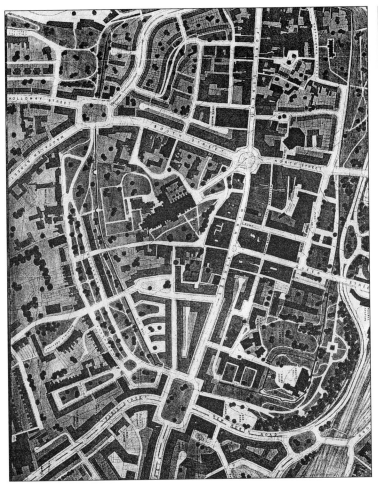

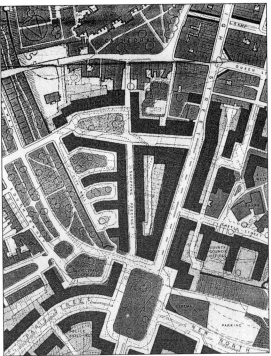

Two early post war plans for the redevelopment of Exeter. Things did not turn quite as intended.

Below: Work in progress on the new Royal Devon and Exeter hospital in 1969. Because of structural faults since then it is being replaced by another new hospital.

Another view of the Royal Devon & Exeter hospital under construction.

This was the little church of St Pancras, Exeter, long ago.

St Pancras church as it is today in the centre of the Guildhall shopping centre.

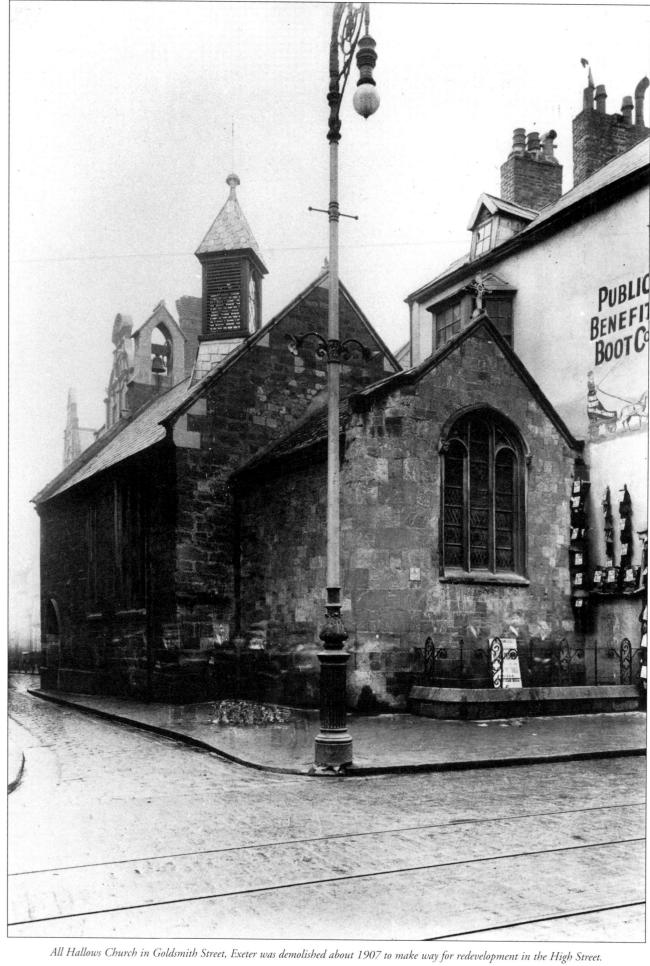

All Hallows Church in Goldsmith Street, Exeter was demolished about 1907 to make way for redevelopment in the High Street.

*Reconstruction work on
Southernhay
Congregational Church,
Exeter in 1957.*

The opening in 1905 of the third Exe bridge. It was replaced after the 1960 flood disaster.

A distant 1967 view of part of Exeter University.

Development at Exeter University in 1967.

One of the many post-war
buildings at Exeter
University. This is the
mathematics and geology
building under construction
in 1966.

This was a terrace in
Northernhay Street,
Exeter in 1958. It
looks much the same
today.

Exeter Cathedral

An old style rally by members of Hoopern Street Band of Hope with the soot-blackened West front of Exeter Cathedral on the left.

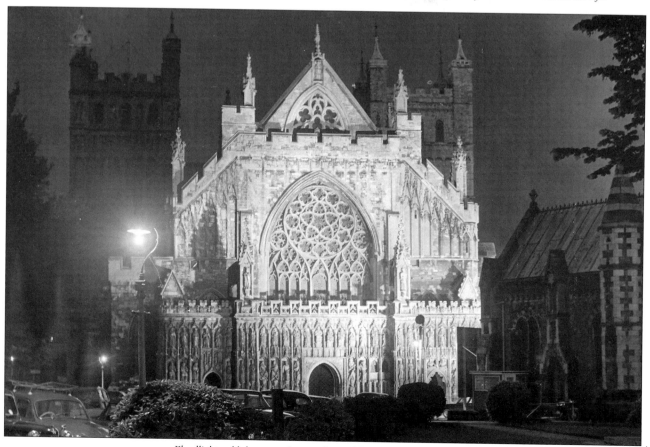

Floodlights add drama to the west front of Exeter Cathedral in 1967.

For 2,000 years these Roman remains were hidden underground in front of Exeter Cathedral. They were discovered in the early 1970s and later the area was filled in again. The Roman relics are believed to extend under the Cathedral. Plans for making them into a major tourist attraction have been debated for several years.

An artist's eyeview of Exeter Cathedral's West front.

The 1953 Coronation Day procession from Exeter Cathedral.

All part of a dog's life in the Bishop's Palace gardens at Exeter in 1960.

The Richard Hooker statue getting a spring clean in 1964. The north tower of the Cathedral is in the background.

Exeter Cathedral's West Front.

Cathedral Close in 1965.

One of the surviving attractive corners of old Exeter in the Cathedral Close as it was in 1965.

Feeding the pigeons on Exeter Cathedral green on a fine day in December 1963.

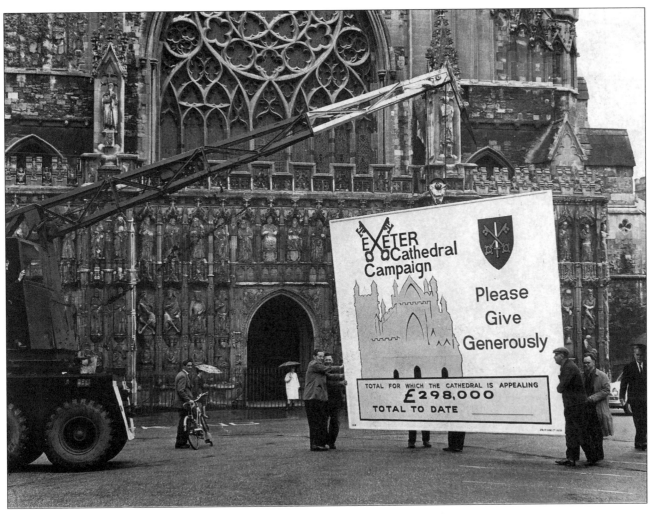

No mistaking the message on this 1966 appeal board.

This reproduction of a water colour picture dates from about 1820 when Exeter still had many surviving gateways. It shows a civic procession in the Cathedral Close.

Mist lends enchantment to this 1957 picture of the Richard Hooker statue on Exeter Cathedral Green.

Police and Fire Brigade

UFOs made headlines in 1967.

Proud members of Tiverton Borough Police force in 1908.

*A police recruits training course at Danes
Castle, Exeter in 1935.*

*Sandy, a very early Exeter police
dog and his handler. The dog was
intended to serve with constables on
the night shift but the only one he
could get on with was PC Charlie
Bullen – pictured here.*

Exeter's first motor-driven fire engine in 1914.

An Exeter policeman giving directions to the Civic Hall in the mid 1930s

An old police pillar on Exeter's Paris Street/Heavitree Road roundabout about 1964.

Bob Shepherd pictured in 1910 with Exeter Fire Brigade's steam operated fire pump.

1934 saw Exeter's first police motor patrol vehicle.

A primitive Exeter fire engine.

Horse-power for the fire engine in St Thomas, Exeter in 1889.

Topsham Fire Brigade in 1927.

Exeter's steam-powered fire engine in 1902.

Entertainment

One of the saddest sights after the 1942 blitz on Exeter was the ruined shell of Dellers Café.

Helen Campbell Russell as a principal boy at the Theatre Royal.

A staff party in the ballroom at Dellers Café in the good old days.

Back in 1957 this was the cast of Robinson Crusoe on stage at Exeter's Theatre Royal.

Merrie England was performed at the Theatre Royal in 1953.

Bertino's Accordion Serenaders who were a star attraction at the Buller Hall in the St Thomas area of Exeter in the late 1930s.

A post World War Two pantomime at Exminster hospital.

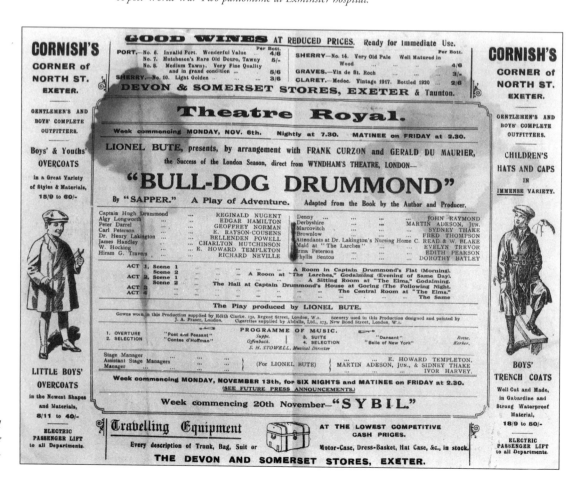

There was more than a Shadow of a Doubt over the future of the Theatre Royal for several years until it closed in 1962.

*Dame Clarkson Rose
at the Theatre Royal
in the 1950s.*

Exeter Silver Band in days gone by.

The Celeste Dance Band at Dellers in 1932.

A change out of uniform for nurses at the old Royal Devon and Exeter hospital when they appeared in the staff panto in 1954.

Back stage with the chorus girls at Exeter Theatre Royal in 1154.

A favourite Exeter band was that of Norman Pincott. This photo was taken in the 1950s.

Head chef George Croft (far right) with some of the 1930s kitchen staff of Dellers.

Neat rows of tables in the heyday of Dellers before World War Two.

Food arrives by car as the kitchen staff at Dellers wait to start on cooking the meals.

The imposing entrance to Dellers Café.

Five months after this picture of a club dance at Dellers it was destroyed in the Blitz on Exeter.

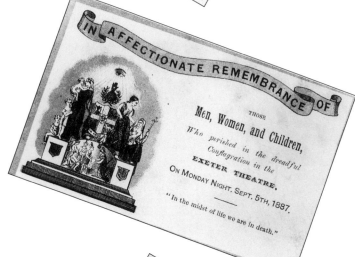

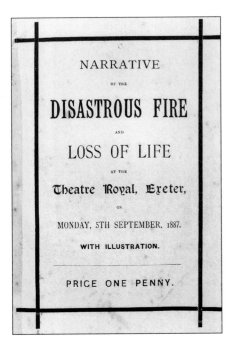

186 people died in the Theatre Royal fire of 1887.

Transport

Thorverton station in its heyday.

Thorverton railway station has been converted into a home.

After Dr Beeching hacked away at Devon's once extensive Rail network some old stations took on a new role. This one at Thorverton became a private house.

An old steam train at Starcross in 1960.

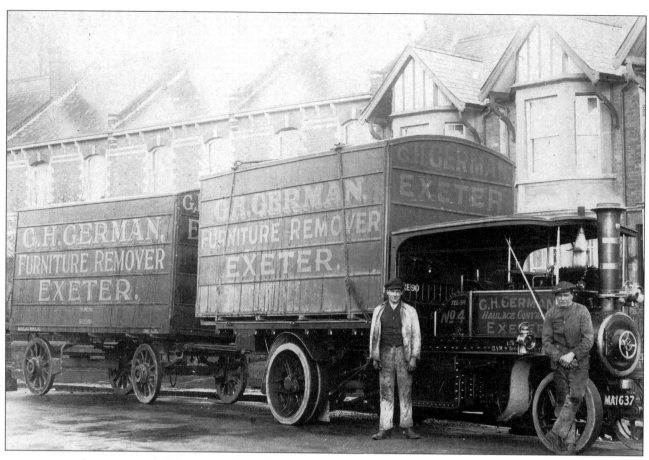

Steam power and solid tyres were features of an early type of articulated lorry used for furniture moving in Exeter.

A classic 1960 Exeter by-pass snarl-up.

Plenty of time for holiday-makers stuck in a 1965 Exeter by-pass jam to buy an ice cream.

The longest Exeter by-pass jam was said to have stretched for 37 miles from Torquay to the other side of Honiton in East Devon.

Newspaper sellers moved faster than the cars in the Exeter by-pass jams of the 1960s.

Traffic jams on the old Exeter by-pass made national headlines for several years in the 1960s.

A wartime collision between a Hurricane fighter aircraft and a car in 1941.

Competitors in the motor cycle reliability trials from Okehampton to Penzance line up for the start in 1921.

Tempers frayed in this kind of traffic frustration on the Exeter by-pass in 1965.

Cars come to a halt as the swing bridge at Countess Wear is opened to let a tanker along the Exeter canal in 1953.

A smash in the early days of motoring at Polsloe Bridge on Exeter's Pinhoe Road in 1920.

Opened bonnets tell the story of overheating on the Exeter by-pass in July 1964.

An open-topped tram crossing the old Exe Bridge in the early years of this century.

A tram accident at Exe bridge in 1917.

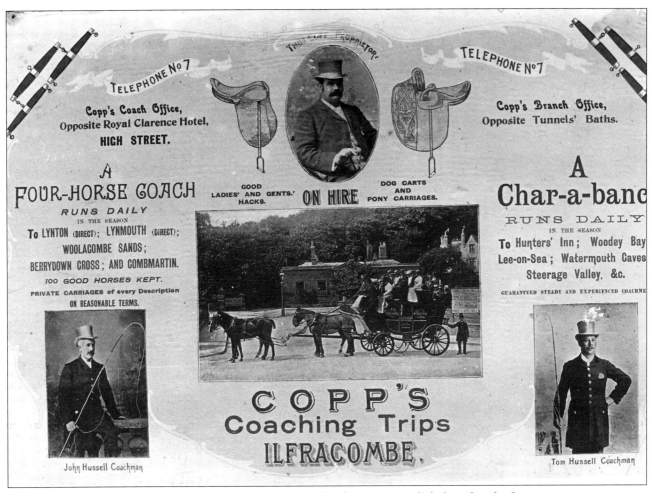

This advertisement of around 1905 for coach trips in North Devon seems a little short of comfort for passengers.

Exeter Guildhall (left) with both trams and horse-drawn transport in the city's High Street.

An old cycle shop in Cowick Street, Exeter.

A once familiar sight as a steam train crosses the bridge in Alphington Street, Exeter.

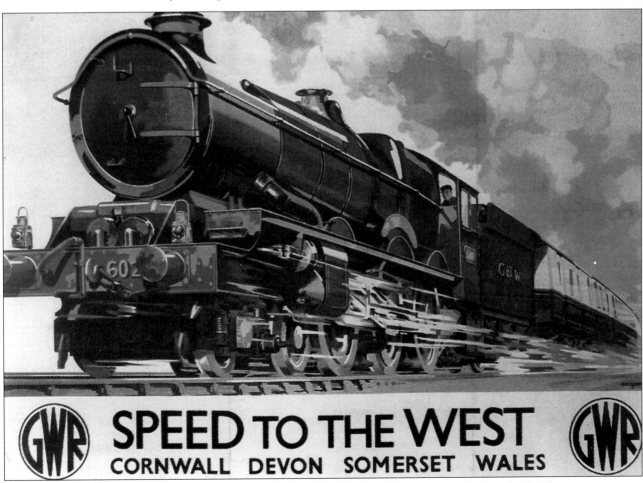

This was one of the old 1930 posters advertising the GWR, affectionately known also as God's Wonderful Railway.

The wooden building on the right was one of several in Exeter used by the police. This was the one in Sidwell Street near the spot where tram passengers could switch to hansom cabs to take them into the city.

The postman at Week St Mary, Henry Gliddon, had a pony and trap to take the mail around in 1890.

An ice-cream salesman of the 1920s in Exeter.

One of the first cars to be driven in Exeter was a de Dion Bouton. This was in the 1880s with wealthy Exeter printer Albert Cannicott at the wheel. He travelled to London to collect the car and drove it back. The initials FJ in the registration number were those of the Mayor of Exeter, F.J. Widgery, who was also a famous Dartmoor artist.

Exeter was once a far busier rail centre than it is now. This was the scene at St David's station in 1906.

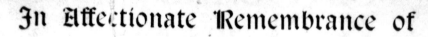

The days of Exeter horse-drawn trams came to an end in 1905.

Flood, Disasters and Weather

Not Venice after dark but Cowick Street, Exeter when the 1960 floods were at their height.

Icicles certainly hung by the wall in the long winter of 1963. This scene was at Longdown near Exeter.

Residents at the College, Ide watch anxiously in 1960 as the stream level rises.

A heavy snowfall in 1963 at Countess Wear.

In 1960 there was too much water for the liking of drinkers at the Bridge Inn (now renamed the Twisted Oak) at Ide near Exeter.

The 1960 floods made short work of this cottage at Alphington. And almshouse residents had to be rescued by boat.

A 1970 snowfall sets off an already picturesque scene at Newton St Cyres, near Exeter.

Surveying the damage to an Exeter street surface after the 1960 floods.

The railway line between Dawlish and Teignmouth is often attacked by the sea as this 1880 picture shows.

Once a place of little bridges and tea gardens, Lynmouth had the heart ripped out of it by a raging torrent in 1952.

A grim photographic record of the mass funeral for victims of the Lynmouth flood disaster in 1952.

Tangled wreckage after the Lynmouth disaster.

Clearing huge boulders brought down by the river after the Lynmouth flood disaster of 1952.

The winter of 1963 was one of Devon's worst of the century. But it provided picturesque views – like this picture of the church of the Holy Cross at Crediton.

The aftermath of a storm at Teignmouth.

1947 brought this spectacular scene into being at the railway tunnel near Dawlish.

Cars in trouble in the snow on Exeter's inner by-pass in 1969.

At its height the Exe was said to be flowing at 40mph down Okehampton Street in 1960.

An anxious time was spent at the Royal Oak, Okehampton Street around Christmas time in 1960. The river Exe was in full spate on one side of the pub and the flooded street was on the other.

A nice verbal and pictorial contrast in Exeter in 1969.

Ivor Doble, well-known Exeter jeweller, looks ruefully at his shop in Cowick Street.

More water than petrol at Pike's Garage in Alphington Street, Exeter. This was in October 1960.

This was one of the Army amphibious vehicles brought in from Fremington in North Devon to rescue people stranded in the Exeter floods.

Dartmoor is a favourite recreation area for Exeter people but not in the kind of weather in this 1966 picture.

In the severe winter of 1947 an appeal was made to save Dartmoor ponies from freezing to death on the moor. Many wandered into Princetown in search of food as this picture shows.

A high tide at Sidmouth in 1961. Since then erosion of its sea defences has become a more severe problem.

Clearing snow from Bedford Street, Exeter in 1969.

Concrete smashed by the sea at Dawlish Warren in 1970.

The little thatched church of St Andrew's at Exton was destroyed by the 1960 floods.

St Andrew's Church, Exton in 1963. It replaced the one destroyed by floods.

After severe flooding at Exmouth in 1963 the Withycombe Brook was tamed.

Crediton has a High Street with a pronounced camber. Snow makes an added hazard.

A snowman made a temporary addition to the scene in Exeter Cathedral Close in 1969.

Water, water everywhere in a 1910 flood at Exminster.

Pushing the boat out at Cowick Street in the 1960 Exeter floods.

Wartimes and Blitz

One house in a terrace at Blackboy Road was no more after a Nazi raid on Exeter.

Battered but still surviving, Exeter Cathedral was framed by gaunt chimney stacks after the Blitz.

Another Blitz victim –
St James' Church, Exeter.

Okehampton Camp, about 1900 (still used today and the start and finish of the Ten Tors Expedition).

A military procession along Market Street, Okehampton c.1911.

One of the mobile first aid vans in wartime Exeter.

A group of Exeter's 'Dad's Army' lads pose for a wartime photo.

Exeter civil defence members on a wartime parade through High Street. Its members saved many lives during the German onslaught that was to hit the city. And in the Odeon cinema, members of the Home Guard got in the act with some novel recruiting methods.

Veterans of the Battle of Arnhem were guests at the first showing of the film Theirs is The Glory at the Gaumont cinema in Exeter in 1945.

Some of Exeter's wartime firemen.

A wartime squadron at Exeter airport.

Officers and NCOs of 'C' Company 1st Volunteers Battalion of the Devonshire Regt in 1888.

1st Exeter and Devon Volunteers on parade in Bedford Circus, Exeter c.1880.

An Exeter citizen kept this poignant souvenir of grim days in World War One.

VE day parade at Exeter Cathedral.

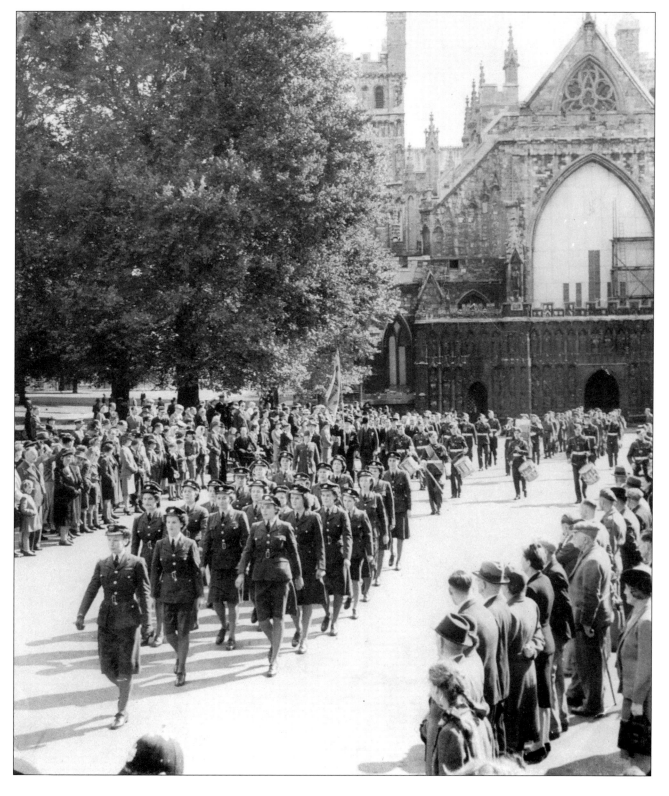

Ansons (sometimes known as flying greenhouses) at Exeter airport before the war.

Some of Exeter 'Dad's Army' in 1944.

A record catch of rats by members of the Women's Land Army near Moretonhampstead during World War Two.

Staff of the Women's Land Army in 1945 at Fairpark Lodge, Exeter.

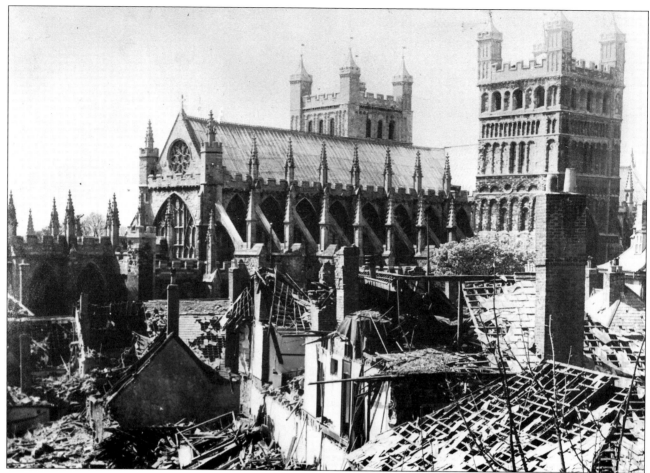

Exeter Cathedral was damaged in the blitz but escaped the destruction that fell upon scores of buildings near it.

Outside Exeter's Wonford Inn during World War Two.

The obelisk in Market Street, Exeter after the blitz.

Contingent from the 1st Rifle Volunteers, ready for service in South Africa in 1900.

Army Pay Office staff in Exeter in 1914.

The end of Dellers café.

Devastation after a night of terror in Exeter.

On the Water

In 1907 this was all that was left of a schooner wrecked at Exmouth.

The demolition of the second Exe bridge.

The old paper mill at Blackaller Weir on the Exe in 1978.

A busy holiday beach at Dawlish Warren in 1969.

A favourite view at Teignmouth – looking across the estuary towards Shaldon.

Youngsters of 1911 dipping their toes in the water at Teignmouth.

Square-riggers in the Dock at Exmouth in 1911.

The pleasure steamer the Duchess of Devonshire beached at Budleigh Salterton in 1926.

Exmouth's lifeboat in 1935 was the Catherine Harriet Eaton.

Battered beach huts after a storm hit the Dawlish seafront in 1969.

Striding along the Exmouth promenade in 1904.

Exmouth pier at the turn of the century.

A 1970 view over the Teign estuary.

The beach at Teignmouth in August 1969.

Swans add interest to the scene near Teignmouth Docks in 1961.

Shaldon Bridge (rebuilt a number of times over the years) links Teignmouth (left) with Shaldon (right). This was taken in 1962.

Sidmouth seafront on a calm day in 1965.

Peaceful waters in Teignmouth harbour in 1967.

Not a model yacht in sight, but plenty of paddlers, at Teignmouth, in 1969.

The old shooting range at Orcombe Point before the present road was built along the sea front. A plan to continue it through a tunnel to Budleigh Salterton was never carried out.

A Dawlish scene was depicted in an old lithograph.

Massive flood prevention work in progress at Tiverton in 1969.

Boating trips in Edwardian days started from near Exe bridge and went down the canal to Turf.

The swing bridge on the Exeter canal in 1961.

Slow progress on the Exe in 1972.

The Custom House & Exeter Quay, from an engraving by W.Spreat, c.1840.

A misty sun over Lympstone mud flats in 1967.

The famous Swan of the Exe with her Cygnet just behind, moored off Starcross in 1922.

Topsham Quay 1900.

Ben Johnson, a tanker in 1955 at Double Locks on the Exeter canal.

Maj David Goddard, who founded Exeter Maritime Museum, with an Ellice Island canoe loaned from Buckingham Palace.

The arrival of the tug St Canute in 1969 was one of the highlights in the early days of Exeter Maritime Museum.

The schooner Result at Exeter's Maritime Museum in 1969.

The Tillerman breaking the ice on her last trip down the Exeter canal in 1963.

The replica of the Nonsuch was an eye-catching sight on the Exeter canal in 1969.

*Old style fishermen at Topsham
show off a record-breaking catch.*

Work on the new Exe bridges in 1968.

Beach scene at Exmouth in 1969.

Seaton fishermen, 1925. Before the 1920s Seaton fishermen caught mackerel and herring in shoals. However, by 1925 the industry was already failing.

A 1969 colony of swans adds interest to the scene near Exe bridge.

An old print of the North Devon port of Bideford.

Rolle canal and aqueduct near Torrington in its heyday.

A scene on Exmouth seafront in the early 1900s.

More rough seas at Dawlish in the early years of this century.

Teignmouth was once described by Devon county council planners as being in the county's 'Bingo Belt'.

A view of Topsham across the water before the Jubilee pier, just visible in the picture, was demolished in 1916 after it became unsafe.

A scene beside the railway at Dawlish.

A misty sunset at the entrance to Exmouth Docks sometime in the 1950s.

These people were looking for a bargain at the Shaldon boat auction in 1966.

Exmouth Harbour was a busy place in 1966.

Feeding the swans at timeless Topsham.

A beach scene at Beer in East Devon.

Exeter Quay and the old ferry boat in the Sixties.

Despite the name on the tarpaulin this was the headless Swan of the Exe, not its Cygnet, in a garden at Starcross in the early 1960s.

A variety of sailing dinghies at Starcross Yacht Club during an event in 1967.

Turf Lock on the Exeter canal looking north.

Mirror images in the still waters of the Exe at Topsham

A new clubhouse was erected by the Starcross Yacht Club in 1966.

*The Topsham
ferry in 1960.*

*Fishing nets cast shadows on the riverside road at
Topsham in 1961.*

HMS Exeter won fame at the Battle of the River Plate early in World War Two. But for many years one of her masts mouldered away in the old Exeter cattle market until it was rescued and put into use as a lever for a lock gate on the Exeter canal.

A view of the old Powderham boathouse which served as a base for Starcross Yacht Club.

There was only just room for the Guidesman to squeeze along the Exeter canal. A picture from the Sixties.

Hard work by members of Starcross Yacht Club as they haul up sections of their new club house in the Sixties.

Neat rows of stooks in the harvest fields beside the Exe in days gone by.

Primitive sea defences at Dawlish Warren in the early 1960s.

Out of Town

Station Road, Pinhoe, at some time at the start of the 1900s.

The Angler's Rest at Fingle Bridge in 1970. This popular pub developed from a booth selling teas about 100 years ago.

A 1969 picture of an angler hoping for a catch from the river Teign at Fingle Bridge.

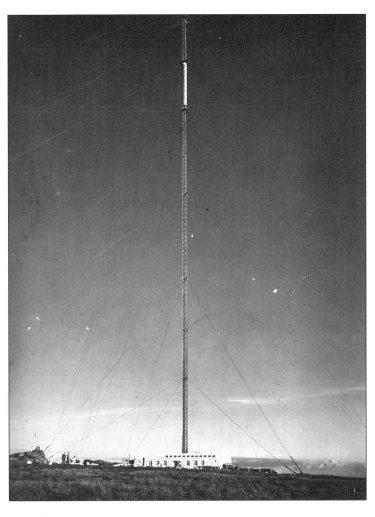

The radio and TV mast at Hessary Tor at Princetown was built in 1963 only after considerable opposition. But for years it has served to bring better reception to people over a wide area of Devon.

Not quite the style of today's ramblers on Dartmoor. This was taken at the clapper bridge at Dartmeet.

The rugged Meldon valley on northern Dartmoor before it was made into a reservoir.

A 1960 interior view at Powderham Castle.

Powderham Castle the family home of the Courtenays – one of Devon's oldest families.

The Saddlers Arms, Lympstone in 1959.

One of Dartmoor's less rugged landscapes.

Woodbury Salterton in the mid nineteenth century.

A hefty Devon woman and a patient horse.

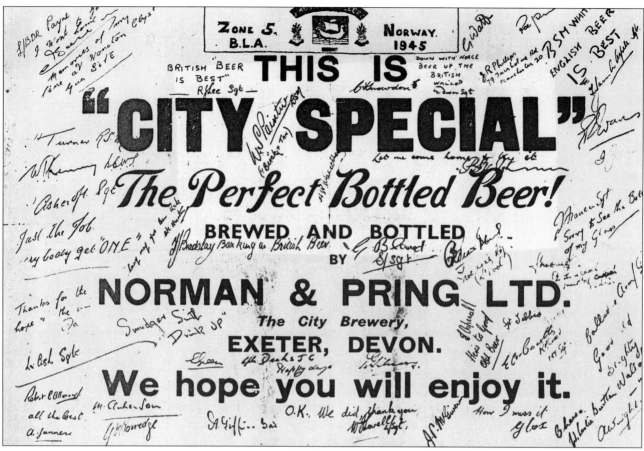

During the war crates of beer used to be sent to our troops overseas. On each there was a large cardboard label to say where it came from. This one was on a consignment sent to members of the Royal Artillery in Norway. They all signed it and sent it back. The original stayed for a long time in the Dolphin Inn at Kenton near Exeter and copies of it were made into postcards.

Old style rick-making at Westacott Barton, Ashreigney.

There were almost as many cattle as people in Okehampton on a day in 1910.

The opening of Tiverton's new bridge in 1968 was quite a crowd-puller.

The Masons Arms at Branscombe, East Devon, in 1959.

Bideford Bridge in 1945.

This church at Honiton was destroyed by fire in March 1911.

A relic of mining days on Dartmoor is Wheal Betsy near Mary Tavy.

One of Dartmoor's seemingly ageless antiquities – Childe's Tomb near Princetown.

The Coronation Day parade at Whipton in 1937.

An old picture of Hayes Barton, the birthplace of Sir Walter Raleigh, in East Devon.

What looks like a spot of dung spreading by women workers on the land near Exeter in World War One.

Women working on the land near Exeter in World War One.

Some pretty big heads at this 1923 Axminster Carnival.

Cathedral Dairy, Exeter

Bicycles at Winkleigh about 1910.

The clapper bridge at Postbridge on Dartmoor in 1963.

The year was 1908 and it was harvest time in the fields at Sandygate near Clyst St Mary when the Hayman family stopped for well-earned refreshments. Grandfather held the horse and Grandmother Hayman kept tight hold of the tea basket.

Old-style fishermen at Topsham.

Stoke Canon, near Exeter, in 1921.

The Warren House Inn beside a bleak stretch of Dartmoor road near Postbridge prided itself on a peat fire that was never allowed to go out.

The Duke of York public house at Iddesleigh, near Okehampton, in 1958.

The Dartmoor Inn near Princetown in 1959.

Old style thatch on the New Inn at Sampford Courtenay in 1965.

There is a fascinating story that goes with the Pack of Cards at Combe Martin in North Devon.

Apart from the horse, wagon and hand cart the scene at the Bridge Inn, Topsham has changed little in the passing years. It is a great favourite with real ale drinkers.

A group of local children filled the foreground of this picture beside the stream which runs through the middle of Newton St Cyres, near Exeter.

Littleham Village, near Exmouth in 1890.

An old corner of Exmouth in 1923.

*Littleham Village, near Exmouth
in 1890.*

*Traditional fun at Hexworthy
Bridge on Dartmoor in 1963.*

Demolition work on a terrace of old cob cottages at Newton St Cyres in 1960.

Whitewashed cob cottages whose doors opened straight on the road were a feature of the winding road through Newton St Cyres until those on the left of the picture were pulled down about 1960.

Newton St Cyres as it was before the cottages on the left were demolished and the winding road through the village was straightened. Replacement cottages were built further back from the road and a village green was created.

A depressing sight for Newton St Cyres villagers in July 1962 when the Crown and Sceptre was burned out.

A group of children at Stockleigh Pomeroy in about 1910. The cottages still look much the same as they did then.

The façade of the Passage Inn, Topsham.

Dartmoor ponies looking for refreshment at
Postbridge in 1964.

Spring 1960 in Ashclyst
Forest near Killerton.

One of Devon's often flooded villages, Clyst St Mary, without a car in sight.

Cullompton Fair in May 1897.

Sport Outings and Schooldays

Not such a happy first day at school for a young girl at Halberton in 1919.

Hoopern Street School, Exeter in 1924 or 1925.

Students at the University College of the South West in World War One. Many years later it became the University of Exeter.

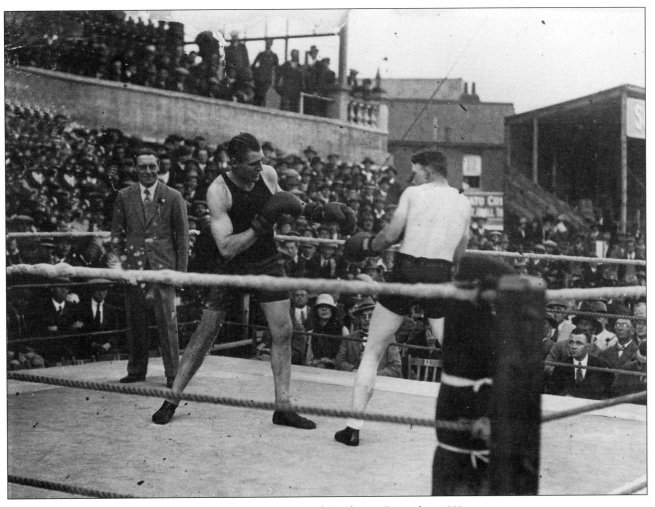

Boxing at the County Ground, St Thomas, Exeter about 1928.

A sea of flat caps among the spectators at a soccer match between Exeter City and Portsmouth.

All dressed up for a turn of the century Devon school trip.

Fancy dress at an Exeter school party in the early 1960s.

Almost a uniform style of hat was worn by women on a World War One outing from Sidwell Street, Exeter.

What looks like an outsize charabanc in Bedford Circus, Exeter in the early years of the century.

A group of Exeter Girl Guides in 1947.

An Exeter shop's staff outing in 1912.

The 1928-29 football team at Ladysmith School, Exeter.

A church outing at Colleton Crescent, Exeter, in the late nineteenth century.

Acetylene lamps and an old bulb horn are unmistakable clues to the date of this Devon pub outing. A man at the back is holding some of the refreshment.

Exeter City Football Club, 1933-34. Back row (left to right): Reg Clarke, Dick Hughes, Arthur Davies, Reg Loram (trainer), Charlie Miller, Jack Angus. Front row: Jack Scott, Stan Risdon, Stan Hurst, Frank Wrightson, Jack Barnes, Harry Webb.

Subscribers

Lisa Abbott
Joan Adams
Michael & Sarah Jane Allen
Becki Almond
Simon Almond
M B Andrew
Mr Charles Atkins (City Guide)
Mr Adrian Paul Autton
Raymond Avery
Margaret Bacon
Mr I J Baker
S E Banbury
Mr & Mrs B W Banfield
R N Barker
Elizabeth Joan Barnes
Miss M Barnes
Mr G A Bartlett
K P Barwick
H F Bealey
Wilred Henry Bealey
Mr R E Beer
Robert Bending
Dennis R J Bennett
Ken Bennett
Ray Bickel
Mrs Betty Bignell
David John Bolt
Mr Raymond Bolt
Mr R C Bolt
R J Botterell
Jennifer Boyle (née Bessant)
Jane & David Bradley
Betty Brenham
John Cannon
Stephen Carder
Ian M Carter
Mrs A E Clarke
Mr Raymond Clarke
Jon Clatworthy
Yvonne Cleave & Family
Mr C J Conibear
Mrs Bernadette Cooke
M J H Cooke
J E Coombes
Richard Cosway
William Cox
Mr C Cumbes
Mrs H B Dark
W Daveridge
Dr John C Davey
N F & P J Davey
Mrs Betty P N David
Miss M Davis
Philip Day
D Dean
Sue Denvir
Miss Marion Dodd
Alan S Dolley

Jean M Doyle
John Dray
Mrs J Drew
Stephen Drodge
Richard Duckworth
Julie Duke
Mr John Dyer
Mrs Wendy J Dyer
Morris Elliott
Ray Ellis
William P Elston
Mr Stephen English
Mrs Margaret Etheridge
Mr Paul C Etheridge
Mr Jeffery Evans
H J A Fernbank
Miss P J Flood
Mr Stephen J Folland
Mrs F Ford
C M Forsyth
Lynne & David Foster
S Fowkes
Mr & Mrs Fowler
L A Freeman
Mr T J Friend
Mr Brian R Gardner
Bill Gates
J W Godd
Audrey Gray
Mrs S I M Green
R W J Greenaway
Steve Grindlay
Miss J Guy
Michael Hall
Mrs E Harbidge
Mrs V E Harrison
Hazel Mary Harvey
Rowan Harvey
Mrs Myrtle L M Hastie
Reginald A Hayman
Alice Hodgson
J A Holman
Hera Holmes
Mrs Mary Holmes
Mrs J Hooper
Mrs J Hooper
Marion Hooper
P R Hoskin
Susan Howland
Robert David Ison
Mr E C Jarman
Arthur Johnson
Mrs B M Jones
Mrs Margaret Jones
Fiona Kelly
Caroline Kitchen
Kenneth J Knight
Mrs P Langdon

Donald W Lashbrook
Mrs S V Lawson
David John Leaver
R G Lockton
Peter Luxton
Mr R E C Mallett
David Anthony Mardon
W J Marsh
Dot and Bernard Martin
Pat Mathewson
Mr & Mrs C K Maun
Mrs M Maunder
Mr G A Mawson
H J Mears
W H F Meilton
Peter Melluish
Mr & Mrs J Meredith
Russell Merrifield
Beryl Miller
Margaret Morris
Patricia Mounce
Daphne & Chris Munday
Mr A Newson
Mr & Mrs B Nicholson
David Norman
Michael Oakley
Trevor Ofield
R D Pankhurst
Mr Andrew W Parkhouse
Mrs Catherine M J Parkhouse
Norman Partridge
Mrs Christine Parr
Mrs Christine Parr
G E Pearce
J C Pearse
Patricia Pearson
Joyce Peeke
Nell Penfold
D S E Perrem
Shirley Perris
'Paul' Perry
Alan Pewsey
Mrs B A Phillips
Jean Phillips
M Phillips
Betty F M Pike
Mr A J Pollard
The Revd. & Mrs Albert Pomfret
Frank Potter
K & J Prance
Eileen Priddle

Deanna Prowse
Vanessa Purchase
Audrey & Edwin Putt
Robert Raw
Mrs L J Richards
Sonia & Mike Richards
Miss Janet Robb
Mrs Joan Rowe
J Rushby
R Sandford
Cyril Sealey
John Selley
Sarah Sheldon
Anne-Marie Sluman
Frances Smith
Mary D N Smith
Mrs G W Smith
Mr David J Snell
B G & F A Sprague
Mrs G J Spray
Mr P Stacey
Edith Stanbury
I M Stapley
Kathleen Steele
Rose Stewart
Mrs B E Street
Michael R Swales
Mary Agatha Violet Stroud
Miss D Taverner
J B Taylor
Rita & Tony Taylor
Karin Thomas
Mr P Thomas
Beenan Treloan
Clarice Tyers
E Urben
S G Vincent-Wyatt
Mr K Vinnicombe
F J Vosper
Lindsay Walpole
C Walton
Albert P Watts
Anne Watts
Mr R G Way
Pam Weaver
Mrs J Wheatley
Anthony William White
Micheal & Sylvia White
Norma Eleanor Whitfield
Mr & Mrs A Wilson
P A Wright